CONTENTS
An Introduction to Bodmin Moor

G000045423

BODMIN MOOR
The hidden heart of Cornwall

Welcome to 'An Introduction to Bodmin Moor'. We hope that by writing this guide, your visit to this special place will be all the more rewarding, and that you will develop an empathy for this wonderful area and share our enthusiasm for what we have come to call 'The Hidden Heart of Cornwall'

It is a special place, rich in birdsong and wildlife, largely unspoilt, despite its industrial past, the remains of which, alongside the many prehistoric sites, go towards creating an exceptional archaeological landscape. It's a place where the pace of life is slow and farming is less intensive than elsewhere in the country. Wild flowers grow in abundance - drifts of primroses in the hedgerows and carpets of bluebells in the woods.

Please help us keep it as you find it and follow the countryside code, a copy of which can be obtained from www.countrysideaccess. gov.uk or telephone 0845 100 3298

If you enjoy walking you may be interested in the four walk books we have published, all based on and around Bodmin Moor. Details are given on the back cover and more information, including where to stay, can be found on www.bobm.info

Stowe's Hill

KNOWING WHERE TO GO AND WHAT YOU CAN DO ON BODMIN MOOR

Traditionally, access on Bodmin Moor has been available via any public rights of way that exist or by permissive arrangement with landowners of the moor. Today much of Bodmin Moor is 'Access Land' where people have a right to run, walk and climb responsibly. It is important to remember that Bodmin Moor is a living, working landscape so please follow the Countryside Code.

For the most up to date information and maps showing where you can go (please bear in mind there may be some restrictions in place), you should visit www.countrysideaccess.gov.uk.

For public transport information call Traveline on 0871 200 22 33 or visit www.traveline.info Corlink is a bus service that operates to the west side of the moor. It must be booked at least an hour in advance. For further information and to book call 0845 850 55 56.

The countryside is a great place to exercise dogs, but it's every owner's duty to make sure their dog is not a danger or nuisance to farm animals, wildlife or other people. Dog mess is unpleasant and can spread infection – please clear up and dispose of it responsibly.

PLEASE KEEP DOGS UNDER CLOSE CONTROL AND CLEAR UP AFTER THEM.

On Access Land, this means keeping them on a lead of no more than 2m long between 1st March and 31st July (the main breeding period for ground-nesting birds) or at any time of year when you are near livestock. Important birds such as Golden Plover, Snipe, Lapwing and Curlew rely on moorland to breed and are vulnerable because they nest and live on the ground.

Do remember that a dog attacking or threatening livestock may lawfully be shot.

Responsible Access

Access Land is for quiet enjoyment on foot and there is **no lawful entitlement** to:
- *ride a horse (unless with a permit)*
- *cycle*
- *drive a motorised vehicle*
- *camp (includes campervans and caravans)*
- *use kite buggies and landboards*
- *hang-glide or paraglide*
- *use a metal detector*
- *take part in organised/commercial games or activities*
- *swim, use boats or wind surfers in nontidal rivers or lakes*
- *remove anything from the area – including stones, fallen wood or plants*
- *dam any rivers or streams*
- *play golf*
- *fly model aircraft*
- *light fires, including barbeques*
- *interfere with lawful activities taking*
- *place or do anything which obstructs or disrupts that activity*
- *engage in any operations connected with hunting, shooting or fishing*
- *kill, injure or disturb any bird, animal or fish*

Delphi Bridge

AN INTRODUCTION TO BODMIN MOOR

Away from the coastal delights of Cornwall sits another area of stunning beauty. Compact in size, though overflowing with things to see and do, Bodmin Moor is the hidden heart of Cornwall. More often than not visitors, and some residents, pass across its wild centre and barely notice it. Others may stop off at Jamaica Inn or visit the prehistoric antiquities, mining remains or geological formations around the village of Minions. Few will ever experience the majestic loneliness of standing on High Moor watching the sun go down behind Brown Willy or Roughtor.

But you do not have to go far to find treasures on Bodmin Moor. Everywhere you look there are prehistoric remains; moorland streams tumble over granite boulders and under medieval bridges, gaunt engine houses, abandoned by Victorian miners, stand sentinel over the moor's edge. Heather and gorse paint the moorland purple and gold respectively whilst the skylark fills the summer sky with his song.

This book has been written to introduce people to the moor. In it you will find information about all the towns, villages and settlements that are dotted across this varied upland landscape. Many points of interest are included, from rocky tors to underground caverns, Neolithic enclosures to 20th century reservoirs. All the places mentioned are accessible to the public and the majority lie within the Cornwall Area of Outstanding Natural Beauty (AONB).

The book is not a walking guide, all the sites featured have grid references and these correspond with both the map in the book and the Ordnance Survey Explorer 109 map. The idea is to go out and enjoy the moor, search out the places featured and perhaps discover new things for yourself.

Whether you are a visitor to Cornwall or a day tripper from another part of the county, I hope that you will find some use for this book and that it will help you to discover one of Cornwall's hidden treasures.

MARK CAMP
MARCH 2009

View north from Stowe's Hill

CORNWALL AREA OF OUTSTANDING NATURAL BEAUTY

Most of the Moor is part of the Cornwall Area of Outstanding Natural Beauty, is legally protected in the same way as a National Park and is part of an international family of designated landscapes. The primary purpose of the AONB designation is to conserve and enhance natural beauty.

The Cornwall AONB was designated in 1959 under the 1949 National Parks and Access to the Countryside Act, with the Camel Estuary area being added in 1981. The status of AONB's was reinforced by the Countryside and Rights of Way Act 2000, resulting in the formation of the Cornwall AONB Partnership and a Management Plan for the Cornwall AONB, produced in 2004.

CORNWALL
AREA OF **OUTSTANDING**
NATURAL BEAUTY

2009 was the 50th anniversary of the Cornwall AONB

HOW TO USE THE A-Z GUIDE

The A-Z guide has been set up to make using this book as informative and straight forward as possible. Each letter has a main heading **1** and entries also have their own heading **2** . If the entry relates to a specific location on the moor there will be a grid reference **3** which corresponds to the Ordnance Survey Explorer 109 Map. Another map reference **4** relates to the map found on the centrefold of this book (Page 38).

1

Gg

2 **3** **4**

GARROW TOR (SX145785) (C4)

Covered in the remains of man's habitation, Garrow Tor is both renowned for its natural landscape and its historical one. Man has lived on this hill for at least 4000 years, his circles, approximately 180 in number and field patterns still discernable amongst the gorse and bracken.

ADVENT (B3)

The parish of Advent lies between the River Camel and Roughtor and comprises of hard won farmland and scattered settlements. At the centre is the church, described by Sir John Betjeman as a "sad little church" (SX105816). Although it is not uncommon in Cornwall for churches to be stuck out in the middle of the parish usually a little community grows up around it. Not at Advent, in fact until the early 1980s it wasn't even possible to get to the church by vehicle and coffins had to be carried over the fields as they had been for the 700 years since the church was built. Nowadays you can park outside and if you are lucky you will find the church open. If so, go in and have a look round, drop some money in the box and enjoy the peace.

Other points of interest nearby:

Long Stone, A standing stone nearly 8 ft tall (SX113820). Tresinney Cross, One of the tallest wayside crosses in Cornwall. (SX105813).

ALEX TOR (SX118787) (C4)

A small rounded tor often overshadowed by its near neighbours Roughtor and Brown Willy. A Bronze Age cairn sits on the summit whilst the rocks that litter the hillside have been sourced for building stone for countless years.

Other points of interest nearby:

Middlemoor Cross, Stands on the ancient route crossing the moor east from St Breward Churchtown. Roughly cut with a very simple cross carved into the head, the stone has fallen at least twice, once in 1873 and again in 1938 (SX125793).

ALTARNUN (SX224814) (G3)

Famed for its church, the pretty village of Altarnun sits just to the north of the modern A30 on the edge of the moor. St Nunn, or St Nonna, after whom the village is named, was the mother of St David, patron Saint of Wales, and it is supposed that her altar is preserved somewhere in the village. The holy well also bears her name, and like the one at St Cleer, is thought to cure insanity. Sadly at the time of writing the area around the well is overgrown and the water stagnant.

Middlemoor Cross

The church is known as the cathedral of the moor and features a Norman font and a wonderful collection of carved pew ends dating back to the 16th century. The original Norman church has long disappeared, the present building dating from the 1400s, its tower rising 109ft over the village. A short distance from the church is the old rectory, famed for being the home of Francis Davey, the vicar of Altarnun in Daphne du Maurier's 'Jamaica Inn'.

Other points of interest nearby:
See TREWINT and FIVELANES

Sculpture of John Wesley over the door of the Methodist Chapel

A bridge over the stream at Altarnun

RIVER BEDALDER

More commonly known as the Warleggan River, this short river rises near the centre of the moor around Temple before feeding into the Fowey in the Glynn Valley. Much of its route is through private woodland but it can be seen in its glory, either at Wooda Bridge (SX147689) or at the 15th Century Panters Bridge (SX159680) which used to carry the main road from Liskeard to Bodmin.

BERRY CASTLE, St NEOT

(SX197689) (E8)

After the Bronze Age, it is thought the climate up on Bodmin Moor became very inhospitable and people moved to lower ground where they were sheltered from the harsh weather. For many years the moors would have only been used for summer pasture or for defence. The remains of the enclosure on high ground above St Neot are said to date from that time, sometime between 400 B.C and 49 A.D. Several hut circles can be found inside the enclosure and although considered to date from the Iron Age it is thought that man was active in the area prior to that time and a defended site may have been here from the Bronze Age onwards.

The views from the top of the hill stretch away to the coast in the south, giving Iron Age man plenty of chances to spot any less than friendly intruders.

The name Berry is said to come from the old English word "Byrig" meaning fort and occurs in the names of several other sites around the moors edge. See BURY CASTLE, CARDINHAM

Other points of interest nearby:

Mutton Down Menhir (SX199695) A large bulbous standing stone built into a wall just off the road.

BLISLAND (SX100733) (B6)

The manor of Blisland, or Bliston, as it was once known, was crown land ruled over by King Harold before he got an arrow in his eye. A medieval manor house still stands on the top right hand corner of the village green, surrounded by many other buildings of historical interest, not least the church. From the outside Blisland Church looks very much the same as any other Cornish church but, once inside, prepare to be amazed. Here on the edge of Bodmin Moor you will find yourself taken back 500 years to before the reformation when churches were full of colour. Not that the décor in Blisland is 500 years old, the rood screen that takes your breath away is only just over a hundred years old, recreated in 1894.

The church is dedicated to St Pratt, although this is believed to be a derivation of St Protus, who with his brother St Hyacinth

The Church at Blisland

were the saints connected to the church since the middle ages. Little is known about them except that they were Roman martyrs and that Blisland remains the only church in the UK to be dedicated to them.

A slate memorial to the Kempe family, who owned nearby Lavethan Manor, can be found in the Lady Chapel. It is crudely carved, the carver having forgotten to put the word "that" into the original line and having to add it later.

One of only a few villages in Cornwall to have a village green, Blisland is a popular spot with visitors. In recent years its popularity has been furthered by the Blisland Inn which, in 2001, was named National Pub of the Year by CAMRA (Campaign for Real Ale). As well as always having a good selection of real ales on sale, the landlord also stocks local cider and serves "hearty home made food" (Good Pub Guide 2004).

Other points of interest nearby:

St Protus Cross, also known as St Pratts (SX104732) Now standing beside the road leading up to the village, this cross lay buried for much of the 19th century. It originally stood near a holy well dedicated to St Protus that disappeared many years ago.

Lavethan Woods (SX100728) These north facing woodlands now belong to the Woodland Trust, but were once part of the Lavethan estate. Traditionally oak would have been the main species growing here, being coppiced for charcoal, building and firewood. Nowadays as well as oak there are beech, sycamore and sweet chestnut plus some larch and Douglas fir, many of which will be removed as part of the trust's management plan to return the woods to their natural state. Several paths give access to the woods for walkers.

BODMIN (SX072669) (A8)

Although not on the moor, the town that now gives the moor its name is well connected with moorland life. The county town of Cornwall for many years, Bodmin is still a bustling shopping centre despite the main county council offices and court having moved to Truro. The Tourist Information Centre and museum can be found in the central square and the old County Gaol can be visited at the top end of the Camel Trail. Lovers of steam can ride on restored trains along two lines to the south of the town operated by the Bodmin and Wenford railway, whilst those with an interest in military matters can visit the Duke of Cornwall Light Infantry Museum opposite the station.

BOLVENTOR (SX183767) (E5)

Known by many only because of Jamaica Inn, the settlement here grew up in the 1840s when a separate parish was created by Squire Rodd of nearby Trewartha (the inspiration behind Squire Bassett in the novel). He built the church and sold off much of the land to form small farmsteads, later building a school house as the population increased. It was this

bold venture to create a community on a windswept desolate moor that gave the hamlet its name.

By the turn of the last century there were over 300 people living in the parish but the hard life and loss of jobs on the land meant that by the end of the 20th century both the church and school had closed and the hamlet bypassed by the newly dualed A30.

Other points of interest nearby:

Jamaica Inn (SX183768) Being on the major route across the moor from Launceston to Bodmin and on to Truro, it is thought the inn existed as a coaching house from at least the 1780s. The inn struggled through the 19th century with several owners and refurbishments until 1880 when it was for sale, but not as an inn. It became a temperance hotel, and was still when Daphne du Maurier visited in the early 1930s.

By the end of World War II it had a club license and was trading as the Jamaica Inn and West Country Club, but it was not long before it had picked up on its new found literary fame and was calling itself "the famous" Jamaica Inn with a Mary's bar and a Joss's bar. There is little evidence to suggest smuggling actually took place at Jamaica Inn, and if it did, the romantic images of illicit brandy and tobacco portrayed in the book and the idea that ships were lured onto the rocks by wreckers, is far from the reality of what really occurred in the late 1700s.

The inn today is still a stopping off point for coaches and travellers, the original building having been extended many times over the years to cope with the number of visitors. Today it also houses a small museum dedicated to the novel and a shop.

See also DOZMARY POOL.

BOWITHICK (SX182828) (E3)

A small moorland hamlet on the narrow road leading down to a crossing point of the Penpont Water. This is a popular spot

Bronze Age burial chamber on the summit of Buttern Hill

on a hot summer's day when children like to play in the stream and walkers go off to explore the rounded hills and tin streaming remains on the north east side of the moor.

Other points of interest nearby:

Bray Down (SX189822) The most northerly hill on the moor and although not of a great height provides great views of the surrounding countryside.from the cairn crowned summit. At the foot of the hill an Italian POW camp was set up during World War II, and in the 1950s the former copper mine known as Wheal Bray was explored in search of uranium deposits.

Buttern Hill (SX175816) Surrounded on all sides by tin stream workings, the whale shaped hill can be a daunting area to walk in on anything but a fine day. Its featureless slopes make navigation hard, but those that reach its summit are rewarded with a wonderful collection of cairns, one of which contains possibly the finest cist (burial chamber) on the moor.

BROWN GELLY (SX196727) (F6)

Overlooking both Dozmary Pool and Colliford Lake, Brown Gelly must have been a very important hill in prehistoric times. Remains of settlements dot its eastern

flanks whilst the summit plateau has five large cairns, the tallest standing at least six metres high and visible from many parts of the moor.

BROWN WILLY (SX158880) (D3)

The highest point in Cornwall at 1377ft (420 metres), Brown Willy is said to get its name from the Cornish 'Bron Wennyly', hill of the swallows. Access to it is easiest (but not easy!) from the car park that serves Roughtor, its near neighbour. Views from the summit cairn are superb, sometimes reaching as far as the coast, both to the north and south.

The summit sits at the northern end of a gently climbing ridge, whilst on both sides the steeply sloping sides have been farmed for centuries, with field patterns and settlements still visible on the western flanks. Away to the east the springs that feed the Fowey River rise amongst marshy areas best left to the horses and cattle to explore.

General moorland view

High Moor (SX163812) Open moorland northeast of Brown Willy. Very rarely visited except by those seeking real wilderness.....or lost.

Butterstor (SX155784) Lying to the south west of Brown Willy, the northern flanks have to be crossed by walkers approaching Brown Willy from Casehill. On its eastern side the remains of Butterstor farmhouse have now stood empty for over 80 years, its yard containing two fine examples of beehive huts dating from the 18th or 19th century and probably used to store food.

In the valley to the east, the flooded works of Wheal Rosa disguise what would have been a hive of industry in the late 19th century when tin was extracted from the alluvial deposits.

CAMEL TRAIL

This popular recreational trail was created in the 1980s after the Wenford lines that ran from Bodmin to Padstow and to Wenford china clay dries closed. The route to Padstow is now one of the most popular recreational routes in the south west, especially for cyclists. However the ex clay line to Wenford tends to be quieter and provides both walkers and cyclists with an enjoyable excuse to get some exercise.

The railway line was created in 1834, one of the first in the world. It was never intended for passengers and for most of its life served the china clay and granite industries of the St Breward area. Nowadays it provides over

6 miles of off road walking, cycling or horse riding on level ground, about a third of the total Camel Trail.

RIVER CAMEL

This is the only Cornish river of any size to join the Atlantic via the north coast and forms the western boundary of the moor as it flows south, passing close to St Breward. Its name has nothing to do with ships of the desert but derives from 'camalan', meaning crooked river. It is renowned for its fishing and, because of this, it is also a popular haunt for otters. These shy creatures have made a successful comeback in recent years and can now be found on nearly every river in Cornwall.

CAMELFORD (SX107838) (B2)

The little town lies just off the northwest edge of the moor and owes its existence to the fact that it was both a market town and an important crossing point of the River Camel on the old road that ran from the west up to Exeter and beyond. Today the main road, the A39, still brings traffic through the heart of the town and over the bridge which many years ago replaced the Camel ford. On both sides of the road there is a good selection of shops and places to eat and stay, information on which can be found at the Tourist Information Centre, situated at the western end of the town in the same building as the museum. Also

Camelford town centre

worth visiting is the old town hall with its golden camel weather vane.

Those who seek some peace and quiet away from the traffic can walk beside the river on a selection of paths on both sides of the town or seek out the parish church hidden away in a valley to the south of the town at Lanteglos. The church is usually locked, but its setting and the collection of ancient crosses in the churchyard are worth a visit.

Other points of interest nearby:

North Cornwall Museum and Gallery (SX104836) An eclectic collection of domestic and agricultural implements fill several rooms in the former coach building works. Upstairs space is given over to an ever changing art gallery. Ring for opening times 01840 212954.

CARADON HILL
(SX273708) (H7)

One of the most well known hills on the south side of the moor due to the telecommunication aerials that sprout from its rounded summit, it also has one of the largest collections of burial cairns in the county. As predominant as they are, the prehistoric remains are over-shadowed by the mining remains that encircle the hill. In 1836 copper was discovered on the lower southeast side of the hill and from this the hugely successful South Caradon mine developed throughout the century.

Reaching a peak in the mid 1850s when over 4000 people were employed in mines around the hill, the name Caradon became synonymous with profits, leading to mines as far away as Camelford using the name to attract shareholders. Villages grew up around the hill, Minions, Crows Nest, Upton Cross, and a railway was built taking copper down to the port of Looe and bringing coal back up.

But it was not to last. By the mid 1880s most of the mines on the hill had either closed or were facing closure, their engine houses abandoned to the elements. Today the area is part of the Cornwall and West Devon Mining Landscape World Heritage Site, its history covered in many books. Although most of the mining remains are on open access land care should always be taken when visiting them as some buildings are unstable and some shafts are still open.

Other points of interest nearby:

See MINIONS

To find out more about the World Heritage Site on Bodmin Moor please visit www.cornishmining.org.uk

CARBILLY TOR (SX126755)

Much quarried hill to the north of the A30 on the west of the moor. Some fantastic

HARD ROCK MINING

Although man is thought to have extracted tin from Bodmin Moor from as early as the Bronze Age, it took the discovery of copper on the side of Caradon Hill in 1836 to make it worthwhile to mine deep into the granite that shapes the landscape. All around the hill and the neighbouring areas mines grew up, some were a success, some failed miserably. Away from Caradon, other mines opened up around the moor; St Neot, St Breward and Altarnun all saw small scale mines open and close during the mid 1800s. By the 1890s nearly all the mines on the moor had closed, leaving just a few that were still searching for tin.

The miners who had moved up onto the moors, from communities all over Cornwall, moved away. Some set sail to find riches across the oceans, from Mexico to Australia. The buildings that had raised so much hope were left to fall back into the rock from which they were built. Today a few stand proud; memorials to a time when Cornwall was a leading industrial centre that sent machinery and men all over the world. The granting of World Heritage status to the Cornwall and west Devon mining areas recognises the achievements made in the 19th century. It will hopefully see the preservation of many of the buildings that remain dotted around the moorland landscape, especially in the Caradon Hill area, and also raise awareness of what man achieved before the days of modern technology.

The Moorland Heritage Centre at Minions, built inside a 19th century engine house.

natural rock formations still exist amongst the four quarries first worked at the very end of the 1800s. Nowadays the workings are flooded, having closed in the 1960s and care should be taken when visiting. Several of the buildings associated with the quarry remain in various states of disrepair.

Other points of interest nearby:

Bradford (SX119755) Described by EC Axford in his book about Bodmin Moor as 'one of the loveliest places on the moor' the little bridge over the Delank River is a pleasant place to spend a hour or so, watching the water run by on its way down to the River Camel.

CARBURROW TOR
(SX156707) (D7)

Situated to the north of the village of Warleggan, Carburrow has been described as an 'insignificant hillock'. This should not distract one from visiting it though, as over 4000 years of history can be explored on its slopes. Extensive Bronze Age huts litter the southern sides whilst the remains of a mediaeval long house can be seen near the boundary wall at the bottom (very near Tor Farmhouse). There are two cairns atop of the tor, the one on the eastern side was hollowed out in the Second World War for the local home guard to use as a lookout post. Archaeologists have suggested that the two cairns were placed on top to model the outline of Roughtor and Brown Willy in the distance to the north, whilst folklore has it that a golden coffin is buried under each, protected by flocks of wild birds.

CARDINHAM (SX123687) (C8)

A parish on the south west edge of the moor centred on the 15th century church, which has a couple of interesting crosses outside. The church serves a scattered community with the largest cluster of houses being nearby and at Millpool to the north. Cardinham Castle to the south of the church was built just after the Norman Conquest and was a ruin by the 1500s. Very little remains to be seen apart from some earthworks in a field.

To the north of the village is Bodmin Airfield, the home of Cornwall Flying Club.

Carburrow Tor, seen across Colliford lake at sunset

Bury Castle (SX136697) An Iron Age hillfort one mile northeast of the village. A footpath runs around its northern edge.

Trezance Holy Well (SX125694) A short distance from the church, the well sits inside a building thought to have been constructed from an earlier chapel on the site.

CARDINHAM MOOR
(SX134715) (C7)

Much of the large open valley known as Cardinham Moor is taken up by the DANGER AREA of the Fore Down firing range. Red flags fly from prominent landmarks when firing is taking place and red and white striped poles denote the prohibited area. The long thin building in the middle of the danger area was a grenade training site dating from just after World War II.

Two former China Clay works sit either side of the danger area. To the east is Glynn Valley, last worked in the early 1940s. The site is still in a remarkable state of preservation with many buildings and settling pits still standing. Avoid exploring the waste tips and flooded pit. Away to the northwest, beside the A30, are the remains of Burnt Heath works, opened in the 1870s and disused by the early 1900s. There is not much to see for the casual visitor and again care should be taken around flooded areas.

Stone quarrying has also taken place on Cardinham Moor with two quarries cut into the hillside on the western escarpment whilst older examples can be seen on Fore Down and at Corner Quoit. The latter, which is now overgrown with lichen covered woodland, may have been the source for the stone used to build the Shire Hall at Bodmin.

St Bellarmin's Tor

Other points of interest nearby:

St Bellarmin's Tor (SX130709) On top of this rocky outcrop stands one of the flagpoles from which red flags fly if the range is in use, although the tor is outside the danger area. St Bellarmin has no association with this area and it has been suggested that the name is a derivation of St Bartholomew, patron saint of nearby Warleggan Church. On the southern slope of the tor are the remains of an enclosed area. This has historically been recorded as a chapel over the years, with a holy well nearby, however there is no evidence to suggest that either existed and it may be just an animal pound.

Colvannick Stone Row (SX128718) As with all the stone rows on the moor, no one knows why they were built. The one at Colvannick runs roughly north south and is made up of stones around 4 ft high. Because of the gorse bushes dotted around the area it is not easy to follow the row but it is thought there are 14 stones in all, spread over 380 metres.

CARDINHAM WOODS
(SX100667) (B8)

A popular recreational area on the south west corner of the moor. Ten miles of trails for both walkers and cyclists wind their way through 650 acres of coniferous woodland. In the centre of the woods can be found Ladyvale Bridge, situated near to the site of a 12th century chapel, whilst high up in the woods to the east sits Wheal Glynn, a 19th century galena mine.

On quiet days it is possible to spot deer in the woods, and buzzards are a common site overhead. However, if you are lucky to spot an otter or a dormouse please tell someone as they are rare in the area, and any information of sightings is much needed.

THE CHEESEWRING AND STOWE'S HILL (SX257725) (H7)

Alongside Jamaica Inn and Dozmary Pool, the most visited spot on the moor must be the Cheesewring. This tower of naturally balanced stones has drawn people to the southern edge of the moor since time immemorial. Although it is one particular tower that gets all the publicity, there are several other "cheesewrings" on top of the hill that are worth viewing. Their origins can be traced back 280 million years to when the granite rock that now forms the backbone of Cornwall and Devon formed.

Cheesewring formations on the summit of Stowe's Hill

Later, when the Ice Ages ended, the solid rocks found themselves standing tall while all the loose rocks were carried downhill with the melting soil. Over the many years since, the wind and rain have eaten into the fault lines in the rock to produce these strange forms. The name "Cheesewring" comes from the fact that the rocks resemble the bags of apple pulp used for making cider. These are known locally as cheeses and, when piled on top of each other in a press, form a similar shape.

The other feature that makes Stowe's Hill a fascinating place to visit is the Neolithic enclosure that surrounds the summit. It is in two parts, the higher and smaller enclosure circles the top of the hill taking in many of the cheesewring formations. To the north of this lies the larger enclosure, on slightly lower ground. Whereas the higher enclosure has no sign of habitation, this area is covered in circles of stone that may have been sites for huts or just clearings for tents. There are also burial sites and a sunken entrance way to be explored in this landscape, which could date back over 6000 years.

CHINA CLAY

China Clay was first extracted from Bodmin Moor in the 1860s. Many of the operations were small and only lasted into the first quarter of the 20th century, the exceptions being Stannon, Parson's Park, Hawk's Tor and Glynn Valley. A man called Thomas Parkyn was responsible for many of the works opening, but their locations far from good roads and ports, meant they rarely made any money.

China Clay is formed when granite starts to decompose, a process known as kaolinisation. To extract the kaolin from the granite, water was allowed to flow over the exposed rock taking the kaolin with it. As time went on the processes used became more modernised and nowadays high pressure hoses are used which blast the kaolin from the rock. It is then piped as slurry to settling tanks, before being dried and graded.

It has many uses, not just for the making of porcelain. Most of the Cornish clay produced now goes to the paper industry, where it is used as filler in the paper itself, and also in the production of the glossy coating found in many magazines.

The last pit on Bodmin Moor to be worked was Stannon to the west of Roughtor. It stopped producing clay in 2000, although work went on re-using the waste dumps for a few more years.

COLLIFORD LAKE
(SX170720) (E6)

During the 1970s arguments raged as to where to site a third reservoir on the moor. Three sites were chosen, the Draynes valley through which the Fowey River flows, the upper De Lank or the marshy area above St Neot known as Redhill Marsh and Colliford Downs. In the end the latter site was chosen and in 1986 the work was finished and the St Neot River dammed.

The reservoir covers a large area and there are several places around its edge where people can park and walk, including along the top of the dam. The waters are well stocked with brown trout, but a permit is needed for fishing (currently available at Jamaica Inn).

Other points of interest nearby:

Penkestle and Letter Moor (SX175703) This rarely visited stretch of open access moorland has evidence of tin streaming which can be seen in the southern part where shallow valleys head westward. More recent history can be found in triangular earthworks, the remains of gun emplacements set up during World War II.

China Clay remains at Glynn Valley

King Doniert's Stone

Fourhole Cross (SX173749 *Standing beside the busy A30, one mile west of Jamaica Inn, this cross is best seen from the comfort of the car as access on foot is dangerous. It was first recorded in 1748 and later authors mentioned that the top of the cross had been shot off by local militia troops. As a wayside cross it would have marked a safe route across the moor in ancient times, a job it still performs today.*

COMMON MOOR

(SX241694) (G7)

A small community tucked away off the Dobwalls to Minions road. Like many of the villages in the St Cleer area, it grew in size during the mining boom of the 1800s, having room for two non conformist chapels, one Wesleyan, the other Bible Christian.

Other points of interest nearby:

King Doniert's Stone (SX237688) *Of the two stones that stand in a little enclosure just off the road, it is the smaller of the two that is associated with King Doniert. The inscription on the stone translates into 'Doniert has asked prayers for his soul' and is thought to refer to a Cornish King who drowned in the nearby Fowey River whilst on his way to do battle with the Vikings on the Tamar River. This would have been the bottom of a cross shaft, but it is not connected to the other stone, commonly known as 'The Other Half Stone'. Both stones feature some wonderful carving and have been here (or hereabouts) together since at least 1600.*

CRADDOCK MOOR

(SX245716) (G7)

Despite being easily accessible from the village of Minions, this ancient landscape is rarely visited by the crowds that flock towards the Cheesewring. Bronze Age barrows and cairns, a stone circle, a stone row and an embanked avenue all wait to be discovered by the inquisitive walker. They do take a little discovering though, all the stones in the circle have fallen over, the stones that make up the stone row are rarely more than a foot high and the embanked avenue can look like any other pile of stones.

What could be one of the most important ritual sites on the moor also includes, just to the north, a large settlement and field system, whilst the remains of quarrymen's buildings can also be found amongst the moor stone. The large quarry on the eastern lip is known as Golddiggings, not because the precious metal was found there but because the granite was of such good quality, it was worth its weight in gold. A track runs out to the quarry from Minions and although a popular place to visit, do be careful of the two flooded workings.

Other points of interest nearby:

Witheybrook Marsh (SX252727) A point of interest but best avoided! The Witheybrook Marsh captures much of the water that flows off the moor to the north of Minions. Closer to the village the stream was worked for tin from the Bronze Age onwards, its man made cutting creating a scar several metres deep. Further north, its deep mire was to be a test for railway engineers in the 1800s, who wanted to build a line across it to connect the south coast with the north. A superb habitat for water loving plants including common and long leaved sundews and cotton grass, which produces wonderful white fluffy heads in midsummer.

CROWDY RESERVOIR

(SX148835) (D2)

Originally planned prior to World War II, this small reservoir covering 115 acres was finally built in 1973. It is a haven for birdlife with a hide situated a short walk from the parking area. Birds known to breed here include Lapwing, Great Crested Grebe and Grasshopper Warblers. The nearby Lowermoor Treatment Works became infamous in 1988, when twenty tonnes of aluminium sulphate were accidentally tipped into the water supply.

CROWS NEST (SX264694) (J8)

A small hamlet lying in the shadow of Caradon Hill and very much the result of the mining boom of the 1800s. The 17C inn, the oldest building in the village, remains as popular as ever, whilst the Wesleyan Chapel, the grandest building ever to be built in the village was sadly pulled down several years ago. A track still gives access to South Caradon Mine, following the same route the miners would have taken 150 years ago, passing as it does, under the bridge of the former mineral line from Minions.

DARITE (SX257694) (H7)

Another village that evolved when copper was discovered in the area. In fact the village was originally known as Railway Terrace as it grew up along the route of the line that ran up to the Caradon mines and beyond. The line crossed the road at the western end of the village, near the turning to Trethevy Quoit, and ran along in front of the houses and school. Situated on a south facing hillside, modern development has taken place at the eastern end of the village, where good views can be had across the farmland of south east Cornwall to the sea.

DAVIDSTOW (SX152873) (D1)

This parish of half moorland, half farmland on the north side of the moor. A series of small hamlets make up the community linked by narrow lanes and un-walkable footpaths. Towering over the parish is the Dairy Crest creamery where Davidstow cheese is produced.

Other points of interest nearby:

Holy Well (SX153874) In a boggy field behind the church sits a rather overgrown well house. It was renovated by a Michael Williams in the 1870s, who it seems took the stone from another nearby well at Lesneweth. The waters are not known to have any healing properties.

St David's Church (SX152873) Sitting all on its own beside the A395, Davidstow Church is well worth a visit. It has some stunning stained glass windows, lighting up what can be a fog bound parish, and a good selection of carved pew ends. The graveyard contains the resting place of Charlotte Dymond, murdered out on the moor in 1844. An information panel in the church recounts the story, which can be found in more detail at the Shire Hall in Bodmin.

DAVIDSTOW AIRFIELD (SX150850) (D2)

Opened in October 1942 to serve both the RAF and USAF, Davidstow Airfield was blighted by the fact that it was nearly always blanketed in fog or mist. Despite that, the US flew Flying Fortresses and Liberators from here and the RAF operated successful air sea rescue duties throughout the war.

At the end of the war, it was decided to close down the airfield and it was left to the sheep and cattle to once again reclaim the moor. That is the scene today, although the forestry has started to encroach on the southern edge, but it is not the whole story. In 1952, Cornwall Motor Racing Ltd was formed with the idea of creating a race track out of the old runways. This was done and several races took place over the next 3 years. Among them were three Formula One races including the first one at which a Lotus was raced. But once again it was weather that ruled the day, that and insurance costs.

Davidstow remains one of the least known Formula One tracks, its airfield buildings stand gaunt against the skyline and it is the creamery that now takes the name forward, the cheese produced there being found all over the country.

Recently plans have been put forward to erect massive wind turbines on land around the old airfield, much to local opposition.

At Davidstow there can be found two museums dedicated to the airfield and Cornwall's role in World War II.

DE LANK QUARRY
(SX103756) (B5)

The precise date of when man first started quarrying granite at De Lank near St Breward is not known but is thought to have been around the mid 1800s. Things developed fast, no doubt aided by rail links to the coast at Padstow and Fowey. In the early 1880s the quarry was given the contract to supply stone for the new Eddystone Lighthouse, and a part of the works are still named after this relatively local job. Further afield many of London's landmarks contain De Lank granite, Blackfriars, Putney and Tower Bridge, The Thames Embankment, New Scotland Yard, The Cenotaph and the Karl Marx memorial in Highgate cemetery, to name but a few. Even as far away as India, Cornish stone found a use; the docks at Bombay (now Mumbai) were built from De Lank granite.

Nowadays De Lank is the only large stone quarry still operating on the moor and it

'Seed', prior to it being moved to the Eden Project

is from here that in early 2005 a lump of granite weighing approximately 180 tons was taken. This was carved on-site into a giant seed, which now takes centre stage in the education centre at the Eden Project near St Austell.

Other points of interest nearby:

De Lank River: Running through the centre of the quarry, though often underground, the De Lank River rises high on the moor in Roughtor marsh. Its course can be viewed at several picturesque spots including both Bradford and Delford (or Delphy) bridges whilst those willing to walk should seek out the falls lying below De Lank quarry at SX101749.

DOZMARY POOL

(SX195745) (E6)

The pool lies in a shallow bowl towards the centre of the moor. These days it can be easily reached by car from the A30 at Bolventor but for many years was a fairly inaccessible place, ripe for inspiring myths and legends, the most famous being that it was the resting spot for Excaliber, King Arthur's sword. Other tales tell of the pool being bottomless, of gorse bushes thrown into it turning up weeks later in Falmouth harbour.

In reality the pool is shallow and has virtually dried out several times over the years. There is also no association with the legends of King Arthur, except for stories written in guidebooks such as this in the early 1900s. At that time it was often quoted that Lord Tennyson had set Arthur's demise here in his 'Morte d'Arthur', although he clearly states that it was on 'a dark straight of barren land, on one side lay the ocean and on one lay a great water', not exactly a lonely moorland pool.

Where tourists now come in search of Arthur, Sunday School outings used to tread, the pool being a popular destination for groups from all over the east of the County. Picnics would be set out on trestle tables and rowing boats took children out to the centre of the pool.

The pool also had an industrial past. In the 1880s an Ice Works was established

Dozmary Pool with Brown Gelly in the distance

here, the buildings on the pool side being the only remaining evidence. Ice was made in the cold winters and then stored in a large covered pit. Later it would be cut up and sent by horse and cart down to the port of Looe to help preserve the fish. The business was not that successful and had closed by the start of the 1900s. Visitors should be aware parking is difficult.

DRAYNES VALLEY
(SX216726) F6)

Saved from flooding in the 1970s, when there were plans to dam the Fowey River at Lamelgate, the Draynes valley cuts through the south side of the moor, forming a natural boundary between east and west. A road from Bolventor drops down into the valley, passing St Luke's Chapel, and following the Fowey River to Redgate, on the Dobwalls to Minions road.

Much of the land in the valley is farmland and has no public access, whilst other areas are boggy and not suitable for walking.

Other points of interest nearby:

St Luke's Chapel (SX195765) Still in use as a place of worship, this small non-conformist chapel was built in the 1890s to serve the scattered community in the valley and around Bolventor. It replaced an earlier chapel built by the Bible Christians in 1858 near to the site of St Luke's Well.

CHARLOTTE DYMOND MONUMENT (SX138817) (C3)

Erected by public subscription, following the murder of Charlotte Dymond beside the

Roughtor ford in April 1844. Her disabled boyfriend Matthew Weeks, was later hung for the crime at Bodmin Jail in front of 20,000 people. There has been much speculation since that he was innocent. A re-enactment of the courtroom drama gives visitors to Bodmin Shire Hall a chance to decide for themselves.

See also Davidstow Church.

EAST MOOR (SX224776) (F5)

This is a large area of open moorland just south of the A30. The main feature is Fox Tor (SX227786) from where it is possible to look out across Redmoor Marsh towards the hills of Twelve Men's Moor. Redmoor Marsh should be avoided, as it is always wet and potentially dangerous. The Victorian author Sabine Baring-Gould found himself up to his armpits in it in 1891, having become lost whilst out surveying the moor.

There are several prehistoric antiquities in the area, including a stone row and a ring cairn. A line of boundary stones separating the parishes of Altarnun and North Hill run from east to west and the abandoned farmstead of Rushyford Water sits ivy covered in the southwest corner of the moor.

Access is easiest from either North Bowda (SX248775) or Eastmoorgate (SX222789)

Other points of interest nearby:

Nine Stones Circle: (SX236782) Re-erected in 1889 by Squire Rodd of nearby Trebartha, there are now only eight stones standing (the central stone is one of the later boundary stones) and all are often surrounded by water. This is the smallest circle on the moor.

Nine Stones circle

Memorial Cross (SX243774) Erected in memory of a Miss Shellaber who died as the result of a riding accident. This modern cross was repaired in 2000, after cattle are thought to have broken the cross off its shaft.

FIVE LANES (SX225806) (F3)

Settlement on the route of the old A30 and once home to a large agricultural market. The King's Head pub , formerly the London Inn, was in 1797 described as 'the best situated inn in Cornwall' and had 10 lodging rooms. It has also been known as The Indian Queen and the Five Lanes Inn over the 500 years it has been here.

FOWEY RIVER (E4-G8)

The River Fowey rises high on the moor between Brown Willy and Buttern Hill. Medieval travellers knew the moor as Foweymoor, just like the rivers Dart and Exe give their names to their respected moors. A natural boundary cutting the moor in two east and west, it runs down through the Draynes valley to Golitha. Here the river increases in size as it flows west along the moor's southern wooded fringe. At Lostwithiel, once an important port and capital of Cornwall, it becomes navigable on high tides. It then snakes between marshland and woods down to the port that has taken its name. Fowey has a deep, busy harbour and a china clay dock, ensuring there is always something going on, a far cry from the wild moorland around the river's source.

To see the river at its best in a moorland environment, either seek out the source at SX170814 or explore north of Bolventor at SX183786.

See also GOLITHA FALLS, DRAYNES VALLEY

Golitha Falls on the River Fowey

GARROW TOR (SX145785) (C4)

Covered in the remains of abandoned habitation, Garrow Tor is both renowned for its natural landscape and its historical one. People have has lived on this hill for at least 4000 years, their hut circles, approximately 180 in number, and field patterns, still discernable amongst the gorse and bracken. In Medieval times, much of the east side of the hill was cultivated, the long

Woodland near Golitha

thin fields heading down slope to the De Lank River. Garrow Farmhouse itself may be of a later date, but in and around it can be found the remains of Longhouses and ancillary buildings .

A footpath runs around the south side of the tor leading to a permissive path across Butters Tor and onto Brown Willy.

GOLITHA FALLS
(SX228689) (G8)

These falls occurs where the River Fowey leaves the granite uplands and plunges down onto softer sedimentary rocks. The name Golitha is thought to mean obstacle, and a large boulder that once blocked part of the river here was blown up in the 19th Century to allow salmon upstream to spawn. Now a popular spot for walkers and strollers, the area is managed by Natural England, who try to keep a balance between a recreational site and an important wildlife haven.

Hidden amongst the ferns and lichens, that thrive in the moist conditions, are the remains of a short lived copper mining operation, known as Wheal Victoria. Two large waterwheel pits sit on the side of the valley at the head of the falls. Nearby, horizontal tunnels driven into the hillside to allow drainage from the mine, are now home to large colonies of bats.

Another industrial feature nearby, is the pipe that once carried china clay slurry from Parsons Park above St Neot, to the clay dries below Liskeard. It can be seen crossing the river only a short walk from the entrance to the woods.

GOONZION DOWNS
(SX175675) (E8)

Goonzion is believed to mean dry place downs in Cornish, so the addition of downs to the name of this area high above St Neot is unnecessary. Crossed by several minor roads, the moorland is covered in shallow pits, the result of miners searching for tin many years ago. It is said that St Neot told his fellow villagers that whoever found minerals up here would become so rich they would be able to shoe their horse in silver. After many failed attempts, St Neot said he would place a white feather on the spot where the mineral lode lay. The following morning the downs were covered in white feathers and that's why there are holes all over the area! Although most of the mining was only done in shallow pits, there were some shafts sunk up here by Wheal Friendship in the mid 1800s, and care should be taken if walking away from paths.

Other points of interest nearby:

Crowpound (SX175677) A rectangular bank to the left of the road near the crossroads. It is probably a medieval cattle enclosure, but legend has it that St Neot sent the crows of the parish here during sermons so that the local farmers had no excuse to abstain. Next to it is an upright stone, which may be a standing stone of prehistoric origin, but could be only a marker stone for the crossroads.

Roman Camp (SX173677) Sitting in a private field just to the west of the downs, the outline of this Romano British settlement can just about be made out from the gateway on the road heading west to Pantersbridge. There is no firm evidence to say the Romans lived here, but local folklore suggests it.

HALVANA PLANTATION

(SX208780) (F4)

One of several large conifer plantations on the moor, planting started here in 1932 and continued into the 1950s. Tracks can now be followed through the mature trees, with little to see except more trees and the occasional deer. Those who go looking for the cross, marked on OS maps at SX208774, will be wasting their time as it disappeared several years ago. A small tin mine in the area worked on and off through the 1800s and into the early 1900s but with little success.

Smallacoombe Downs to the south is another plantation, now in the process of being cut down. This is leaving an ugly scar on the landscape, the large ridges and furrows showing how the industry changes the topography. It is hoped in the future that this area will revert back to open moorland.

HAWK'S TOR (SX142756) (H5)

This is one of many small rock crowned summits on the moor, and one of two called Hawk's Tor (the other is part of Twelve Men's Moor). The name is associated with the disused China Clay pit beside the A30 as you climb eastwards toward Jamaica Inn. Production ceased here in 1971 and the flooded pit is now used as a back up for Colliford Reservoir to the south.

Other points of interest nearby:

Trippet Stones (SX132750) One of the most accessible stone circles on the moor, being reached easily from the minor road across Manor Common. Of the 27 stones that originally made up the circle, only 12 remain, and some of them are lying flat in the ground. Work has been carried out over the last few years to repair damage caused by animals that create pits around the stones (see Nine Stones on East Moor). The central stone is a later addition to the circle and has the letters M and C carved into it, marking the boundary between land owned by Lords Clinton and Molesworth.

HENWOOD (SX266734) (H6)

It is difficult to realise nowadays, but this small village was once at the centre of the industrial revolution. Around 150 years ago, up to 12 engine houses belched smoke from the hillside to the south, machinery toiled all day, clanking and banging, and disease was rife in what would have been little more than a shanty town. Nowadays the village is quiet, with pretty miners' cottages and the former chapel all converted into modern dwellings.

To get some idea of what life was like in this area during the mid 1800s, read the novel 'Catch the Wind' by EV Thompson. It tells

The village of Henwood sits in the dip below Stowe's Hill

ever way you approach it, the summit rocks gain in magnitude the further west you go. At the far west end, a Cheesewring style tower of rocks, looks almost ready to fall as it hangs over the surrounding moorland. Just a little further on, the final few yards of the railway line that climbed all the way from Looe on the south coast, ends amongst the scattered rocks. Stone from here was taken by rail to be shipped all over the world, and the route of the railway can be seen crossing the moor to the south of the tor.

of the trials and tribulations of a miner's life here in the village and up at nearby Sharptor. It also won an award in 1977 for best historical novel.

Kilmar Tors rock strewn north face

On the northern flanks of the hill, often in shadow under the towering crags, can be found several Bronze Age cairns complete with cists, small stone lined burial chambers. Nearby, on private land belonging to Trewortha Farm, three Bronze Age huts have been recreated.

KILMAR TOR (SX253749) (H5)

Towering over Twelve Men's Moor, this half mile long ridge is the highest point on the south side of the moor. Impressive which

KING ARTHUR

It is easy to understand how Bodmin Moor became associated with the legends of King

Arthur; its windswept featureless uplands must have been just what the writers of old were looking for, when searching for inspiration as they retold the stories.

The first mention of King Arthur and Bodmin Moor is thought to come in the mid 12th century, when a man known only as John of Cornwall claimed to have translated some ancient Cornish manuscripts known as the 'Prophesy of Merlin'. In it, the moor is known as 'Brentiga', known by the Saxons as 'Fowey Moor'.

In 1610, the map maker John Norden included in his Historical Description of Cornwall, a drawing and report of King Arthur's Hall, an enclosure high on the moor to the west of St Breward. Arthur would also

later become associated with the rocky Trewortha Tor, where a series of rock basins take the name King Arthur's Bed.

In the 1800s, the moor's closeness to Tintagel twice brought Lord Tennyson to the area, the first time in the company of the Rev Hawker of Morwenstow in North Cornwall. Hawker himself was to link the moor with Arthur in his epic poem 'The Quest of the Sangrall', whilst Tennyson's poetry was to be linked, perhaps unintentionally, with Dozmary Pool. At Slaughterbridge, to the north of Camelford, an inscribed stone is said to mark where Arthur fell in his last battle, an event re-enacted for fans of the legend in the area each year.

King Arthur may be fact or fiction, but his

King Arthur's hall

legacy brings many to Cornwall every year. Whether he ever rode across Bodmin Moor with his knights is open to question but it is easy to see how the inspiration for many of the tales could have come from the open moorland and rugged crags.

See also DOZMARY POOL

KING ARTHUR'S HALL
(SX129776) (C4)

Easily reached from the road at Candra, this enigmatic earthwork sits high on the windswept King Arthur's Downs. Experts have long discussed what it was used for and when it was built. A prehistoric henge or a medieval animal pound being the two ideas usually put forward. Rectangular in shape with a stone lined bank surrounding a boggy centre, it is best visited in late spring or early summer when the cotton grass is in flower. The remains of two stone circles can be found just to the east of the hall at SX134775.

L

LESKERNICK (SX184804) (E4)

Visitors to this area must be prepared to walk some distance over rough moorland,

but will be rewarded with a landscape full of history. The hill itself is covered in the remains of a Bronze Age settlement, whilst on the valley floor to the south there are two stone circles and a stone row. To the north and east, evidence of tin streaming can be seen in the cuttings along the valley floor, the workings to the north being some of the deepest on the moor.

Ancient field boundary's at Leskernick

Leskernick Farmhouse, sitting down beside the ever evolving Fowey River, must be one of the most isolated homesteads still inhabited on the moor. A track from Westmoorgate cuts through the peaty soil, allowing access for the owners' four wheel drive vehicles only.

LISKEARD (SX252645) (G9)

A market town to the south of the moor that expanded rapidly after copper was discovered on Caradon Hill in the 1830s. From the early 1300s onwards, miners had brought tin to the town, where it would be

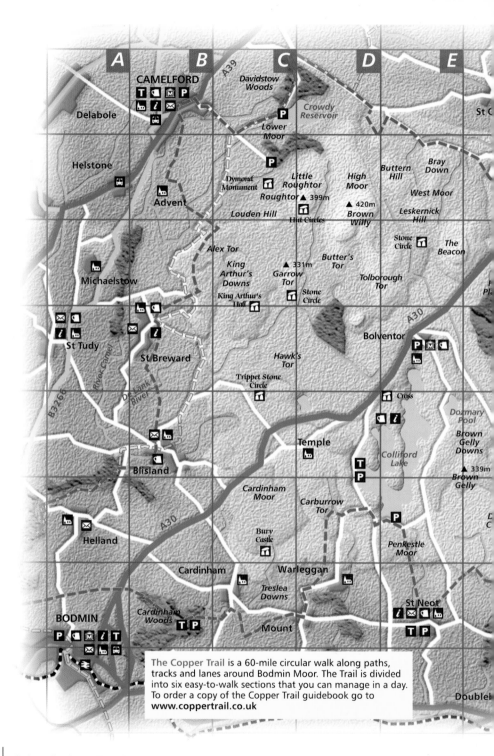

The Copper Trail is a 60-mile circular walk along paths, tracks and lanes around Bodmin Moor. The Trail is divided into six easy-to-walk sections that you can manage in a day. To order a copy of the Copper Trail guidebook go to **www.coppertrail.co.uk**

F A395 **G** **H** **J** **K** **L2**

Laneast

Pipers Pool

Tregadillett

Trewen

A30

LAUNCESTON

3

South
Petherwin

Altarnun

Lewannick

4

B3257

B3254

Fox Tor

Larrick

East
Moor

North
Hill

Coad's
Green

5

Hawks
Tor

Trewortha
Tor

Twelve
Men's Moor

B3252

Kilmar Tor

Smallacoombe
Downs

Langstone
Downs

Notter
Tor

Rilla
Mill

Bray Shop

6

Siblyback
Moor

Sharp
Tor

Henwood

Linkinhorne

Stowe's Hill
381m ▲

Stowe's Pound

Pheonix Mines

River Lynher

Cheesewring

Craddock
Moor

The
Hurlers

Upton
Cross

7

Fowey

Tregarrick
Tor

Minions

Siblyback
Lake

Caradon Hill
▲ 369m

Trevigro

Common
Moor

Cross

Pensilva

Darite

8

Trethevy
Quoit

King Doniert's
Stone

Tremar

St Ive

A390

St Cleer

olitha
Falls

St Cleer
Downs

9

LISKEARD

i Tourist information		▬ ▬ ▬ The Copper Trail	
Bus stop		▭ ▭ ▭ National Cycle Route	
P Car park	**Church**	**Historic site**	
T Toilets	**Watersports**	**M** Museum	
Pubs & inns	**Post Office**	**Railway Station**	

A-Z Guide to Bodmin Moor | **39**

tested, valued and sold. By the mid 1400s the town is said to have been the second richest in Cornwall, the richest being Bodmin.

One building that may have been standing during those early boom years is Stuart House, at the bottom end of The Parade, the large open street at the top of the town. Much modified over the centuries, it is now an art and heritage centre, well worth a visit, as is the town's museum, housed in the Foresters Hall on Pike St. Alongside the museum is the Information Centre, here you will be able to find leaflets and books about Bodmin Moor and source accommodation.

The moorland farmers still visit the town on Thursday, when the local livestock market is held, and the town is the main shopping centre for many on the east side of the moor.

LISKEARD AND CARADON RAILWAY

This was built in the 1840s to serve the mines and granite quarries of the Minions area. Heavy wagons full of stone and ore would use gravity to run down from the moor to Moorswater below Liskeard. There the cargo would be transferred onto barges before making its slow journey down the six mile long Liskeard and Looe Canal.

With mining production intensifying the canal company took the decision to build a railway alongside the canal in the 1850s

and shortly after this an extension to the mineral line up onto the moors was diverted around Caradon Hill. This allowed steam trains to access the mines and the steep stretch just south of Minions known as the Gonamena Incline was abandoned.

Following the closure of most of the mines in the area by the late 1800s, the railway struggled on. Granite was still being quarried and sent out from the port at Looe and the occasional Sunday school excursion brought children up onto the wild moors. But the outbreak of war in 1914 signalled the end of the line and much of it was taken up and sent out to the battlefields of France. Its serpentine course can still be traced in and around the village of Minions and Caradon Hill, where granite setts remain in place, handy stepping stones when the ground is wet and muddy.

LOUDEN HILL (SX137804) (C3)

The Logan Stone on Louden Tor

Dwarfed by its near neighbour Roughtor, Louden Hill sits adjacent to the man made hills of the former china clay works at Stannon. Bronze Age cairns and settlements can be seen on its southern flanks, whilst the remains of a medieval longhouse can be found facing Roughtor. At the northern end of the summit ridge a large logan rock can be found, this is a rock that can be rocked by only a small amount of effort from a passing walker.

Mm

METHODISM

All across the moor are small chapels, built mainly in the 1800s, to serve a community that had adopted the non conformist views of John Wesley. He had originally visited the moor in the 1740s, and initially was not welcomed. However, his open air preaching soon gained in popularity and small places of worship were created in barns and even moorland cottages. As Methodism grew so did the demand for larger meeting places and all over the moor chapels began to be erected. Many of these were small, just big enough to support the community. In larger towns, especially those where mining was the prevalent employer, grand buildings were built to rival the parish church or, as in Pensilva, the chapels came before the church.

Breakaway sections then developed amongst the Methodists and so, in some communities, you will find not only a Wesleyan Methodist chapel but also a Bible Christian one, a Primitive Methodist, a Free Methodist, an Ebenezer, Zion and then, finally, as populations and congregations dropped, a United Methodist Chapel.

Nowadays, many of the moorland chapels have closed and been turned into private homes, but some remain. At Highertown in Advent parish, the tiny chapel set up for the china clay workers in nearby Stannon Pit is still open even though the pit has closed. In Blisland, the small congregation moved back into the 1837 chapel after the new larger chapel, built in 1880, was sold off in the 1960s and converted into a house.

Abandoned chapel in the Draynes Valley

Both of these buildings are some way from the village centre, as was often the case as local landowners were very much church goers and would not let the non conformists build on their land.

See also: Pensilva, Trewint, St Cleer

MINIONS (SX262812) (H7)

If you look on the original OS maps of the early 1800s you will find no trace of Minions, it didn't exist. It was only with the discovery of copper on nearby Caradon Hill in the 1840s that people started to populate this high moorland area. Even then the name Minions didn't exist, the village being known as Cheesewring Village into the early 20th century.

That's not to say people had not lived here before. The surrounding moorland is rich in the remains of prehistoric life dating back to Neolithic times when people chose Stowe's Hill to the north of the village for a large encampment.

The village itself centres on the Cheesewring Hotel, Post Office/General store and Hurlers Halt tea shop. All offer refreshments for the needy walker. At one time the railway ran straight through the centre of the village, now you are more likely to see sheep or cattle strolling along the road, oblivious to modern traffic. It is a reminder, if needed, that you are on the moor proper here, no enclosed fields just open moorland stretching away, waiting to be explored.

Other points of interest nearby:

Long Tom Cross (SX256706) Marked on OS maps, to the west of Minions, as The Longstone. This stone stands just south of the road. Like many of the other crosses on the moor it would have been used to guide travellers in the days before road signs and maps. It is believed that the cross was carved in the 10th century onto an earlier standing stone, probably over 3000 years old.

The Hurlers (SX258713) A unique triple stone circle, steeped in mystery and folklore. Legend has it that the stones are the forms of people turned to stone for playing the game of hurling on the Sabbath. Hurling is a game similar to rugby but without the rules, still played in the Cornish towns of St Ives and St Columb. Two other stones lie just to the west, called the Pipers, they are supposedly the musicians playing whilst the game took place.

Miners cottages line the road at Minions

In reality the stones were originally erected sometime in the Bronze Age, but for what reason is not known. The southern circle is the least complete, with very few stones standing whilst the other two circles show signs of modern re-erection of the stones, a concrete base clearly viewable on one stone.

Rillaton Barrow (SX260819) To the north of the village sits a large uneven mound, which often features pools on its summit. This is a Bronze Age burial site, randomly dug into in the mid 1800s by miners supposedly looking for building stone. What they found was not building stone but one of the most treasured discoveries of British history, the Rillaton Cup. A gold cup, just over 8cms high, it was initially given to King William IV but later disappeared, eventually turning up in King George V's dressing room where he used it to keep his cufflinks in. In 1936 it was presented to the British Museum, but a copy can be seen in the Royal Cornwall Museum in Truro.

The chamber in which the cup was found was rebuilt in the early 1900s and can be found at the east end of the barrow. On some days it is possible to look inside and see phosphorescent moss growing on the walls.

See also; Caradon Hill. The Cheesewring, Craddock Moor, Liskeard and Caradon Railway, Tregarrick Tor.

MOUNT (SX146680) (C8)

A small linear village on the old coach road from Liskeard to Bodmin. At one time the village boasted two shops, two butchers, a carpenter's shop and sawmill, an undertakers, a blacksmiths, a school and a pub, all no doubt as a result of the employment provided by the Wheal Whisper mine at nearby Warleggan. But sadly now, all that remains is a plaque on the wall of the cottage which used to be the Soldier's Arms and the sign above the schoolhouse. Part of Warleggan Parish.

Other points of interest nearby:

Panter's Bridge (SX159680) Dating from the 15th century, this two arched bridge over the Bedalder River was bypassed in 1968 by a modern bridge, a few yards downstream.

Welltown Inscribed Stones (SX136678) Two stones stand high up on the bank at this isolated crossroads. By midsummer they are engulfed by the flora, but a visit beforehand will reveal faint Latin inscriptions, one of which is thought to be to refer to a Bishop Titus. They probably date from sometime between 500 and 1000AD.

NORTH HILL (SX273766) (H5)

Small village sitting above the Lynher Valley on the east side of the moor. Its church, dedicated to the unknown St Torney, was built in the 14th century although much of what can be seen was added later. Around the church there are some interesting cottages especially on the east side and running down to the Racehorse Inn, which was formerly a school.

Other points of interest nearby:

Trebartha (SX265774) The road north from North Hill passes through the hamlet of Trebartha with its tidy cottages and outbuildings. These were once part of the large Trebartha estate, the glory days of which have long gone. It was acquired by a Norman knight shortly after the conquest and had passed by marriage or will down to the Rodd family who finally sold the estate in 1940. Squire Rodd was almost certainly the inspiration for Squire Bassett in du Maurier's "Jamaica Inn".

Trebartha Hall stood in the valley below the road, but was demolished after World War II. It had been used as a military hospital and to house refugees and it is said that it when they left it was in such a state that it was easier to pull down than to repair.

Since 1940 when the Latham family bought the estate, it has been primarily run as a forestry based concern, hence all the fir plantations on this side of the moor. The grandeur of the original hall can only be guessed at, but if it is anything like the buildings that flank the road going through the hamlet, it must have been a fine house.

PENDRIFT DOWNS

(SX105745) (B6)

An area of open moorland between Blisland and St Breward, dropping down to the DeLank River. The north facing slopes are covered in ancient woodland rich in lichens and mosses, whilst the more open hillsides are carpeted in bluebells in the spring. The southern part of the downs provide accessible level walking amongst gorse bushes but can be difficult to route find in.

Other points of interest nearby:

Jubilee Rock (SX104744) This large lump of granite was first carved in 1810 to mark the golden jubilee of King George II. A carving of Britannia adorns the front of the rock, whilst around the sides are the coats of arms of various Cornish nobility. In the late 1800s, more carving was added to celebrate Queen Victoria's golden jubilee.

The rock is not always easy to find, depending on which direction you approach it from, but is worth seeking out. The views from on top on a fine day are superb.

PENPONT WATER (D3)

More a tributary of the River Inny than a river itself, the Penpont rises in the heavily tin-streamed valleys to the north and west of Buttern Hill. Flowing east from Bowithick, it follows the edge of the granite before passing through Altarnun to join the Inny at the A30, just south of Polyphant. It can be seen at its best at Bowithick, whilst picnicking beside the stream or below the church in Altarnun.

PENSILVA (SX293698) (J7)

Another of the villages that appeared because of the mining boom around Caradon Hill in the mid 1800s. In the 1840s the only habitation in the area, then known as Silva Down, was Bodminland Farm but this was soon to change. Almost overnight the miners moved in and rows of cottages were erected. By the mid 1870s there were around 2000 people living in the village with 360 children of school age, a population greater that some of Cornwall's main towns. Three non conformist chapels were built and a pub, The Victoria, for those not so non conformist.

The small mission church of St John was built in 1900 from funds bequeathed from the will of a recently deceased vicar of the parish; its main aim was to bring some of the non conformists back to the Anglican Church.

The village today is a mixture of old and new. The original miners' cottages are still there but another massive expansion during the 1960s and 70s saw many new houses built at either end of the village. All of the non conformist chapels have closed, although the church stays open and a new community centre was opened to celebrate the millennium.

Other points of interest nearby:

Fore Down (SX278693) This large, gently sloping open area to the south of Caradon Hill is a popular recreational space. During World War II it was used to grow vegetables to supplement the war effort.

PHOENIX UNITED MINE

(SX264725) (H7)

Little remains to the untrained eye of what was the largest mine in the Minions area, except for the odd pile of masonry covered in cotoneaster. Sloping northwards, the lower part, rich in heathers, gorse and rhododendron bushes, contrasts heavily with the barren wasteland seen at the top. Here nothing grows on the mineral rich waste tips where amateur geologists can sometimes be seen hunting for treasures. Collapsed shafts across the area have been fenced off in recent years, but it is still best to keep to clear paths.

The area is now a site of special scientific interest (SSSI) and is home to mosses that grow nowhere else in the world, as well as colonies of bats that nest in the adits draining the abandoned mines. The former Counthouse, home of the mine manager, sits at the top of the site in private grounds.

PRINCE OF WALES ENGINE HOUSE

(SX265722) (H7)

The Prince of Wales Mine was built in 1907 to tap into the by then closed down Phoenix mine. In June 1909 the huge beam engine began pumping and great hopes were expressed for a new era in mining on the moor. Sadly, although much money was spent on building the mine, no ore of any value was brought out and by 1914 it had closed never to reopen. Over the last 15 years or so the buildings have been tidied up and made safe and the area is now one of Cornwall's Mining World Heritage sites. It allows the visitor to see not only the tall engine house, but also the boiler houses, winding house and the building where air was compressed to be sent down the mine to power the tools.

Prince of Wales engine house

RIVER INNY (D1-F2)

With its headwaters in Davidstow parish this river, also spelt Inney, drains the very north of the moor. It is at its most picturesque around St Clether where it runs beneath rocky crags before joining the Penpont Water and flowing into the Tamar on the county boundary.

RIVER LOVENY (E7-8)

Also known as the St Neot River, the construction of Colliford Reservoir in the 1980s foreshortened the river to only around four miles long. It joins the River Fowey at Twowatersfoot in the Glynn Valley having passed through the deep wooded valley below St Neot, where it carves a route through abandoned slate dumps and quarries.

RIVER LYNHER (H5-L9)

If the River Camel is the guardian of the western moor, then the Lynher is the guardian of the east side. Forming on the high ground to the west of Trewint, it flows along the edge of the moor passing beneath North Hill where its chief tributary, the Witheybrook, joins it. Ever widening, it heads off into the prime Cornish farmland before joining the sea in Plymouth Sound.

The name is said to derive from "long lake" or "lake like" depending on which book you read. The river's wide but shallow course is popular with fishermen with Atlantic Salmon, Brown and Sea Trout present.

The best place to view the river is beneath North Hill where several footpaths cross the river on bridges, or between Rilla Mill and Starabridge where several footpaths hug the bank.

RIVER SEATON (J8)

Not really a moorland river, its source being amongst the mine workings of Caradon Hill, this small river was very important in the heyday of the mining industry. Initially it would have been used to wash out the alluvial deposits of the early stream workings then, years later, used to power waterwheels in the valley floor where the ore was processed.

It still runs down through the remains of the South Caradon Mine dressing floors, before passing through Crows Nest and Rosecraddock Manor to reach the sea at the village that takes its name, just east of Looe.

ROUGHTOR (SX145808) (D3)

Roughtor stands about 60 ft lower than its neighbour Brown Willy but often looks the more impressive of the two with its rugged crown of granite reaching up into the sky. Visitors should remember that Rough is pronounced row as in cow, just as Fowey is pronounced Foy!

The main summit rocks shelter the medieval remains of St Michael's Chapel and a memorial to the 43rd Wessex Division who served in the North West European campaign 1944-45. Part of the tor belongs to the National Trust, one of the few bits of Bodmin Moor not in private hands.

On the hill's western flank, and passed by most of the visitors who tramp up from the car park, are the remains of a Bronze Age settlement with hut circles and enclosures clearly visible. The walk up from the car park can be steep in places, and may include some scrambling over low rocks

General moorland view

near the summit, but don't let this put you off - the views on a fine day are some of the best in Cornwall.

Other points of interest nearby:

Showery Tor (SX149813) At the northern end of the Roughtor ridge, this little tor has at its centre a Cheesewring type rock formation surrounded by a cairn of stones. This is regarded by those in the know as a very important site in prehistoric times. Between the tor and the car park is an embanked avenue, one of only two on the moor, and excavated by Channel 4s Time Team programme in 2007.

Roughtor from the east

Fernacre Stone Circle (SX145800) On flat land directly to the south of Roughtor, this large circle can be viewed from the summit or seen close up by following the track from Middlemoor Cross.

Ss

SHARP TOR (SX261737) (H6)

Looking like a mini mountain when approached from the Minions Henwood road, Sharp Tor's height is amplified by the way it climbs out of the surrounding countryside. From the summit on a clear day, it is possible to see Lundy Island and the early warning station at Morwenstow on the north Cornish coast.

The hamlet that lies below was once home to the author EV Thompson who based his novel 'Chase the Wind' in the area, the mine at Sharptor taking centre stage.

A prehistoric field system can be seen in the fields between the tor and the village, the diagonal earth banks standing proud but best viewed from Stowe's Hill on a summer's evening when shadows are long.

Sharptor rises over fertile farmland on the edge of the moor

SIBLYBACK RESERVOIR

(SX235709) (G7)

Completed in 1969 and covering 140 acres, Siblyback is the South West Lakes Trust's main activity centre on the moor. Here, visitors can canoe, windsurf or sail, whilst fishermen prefer to spend the day trying to lure rainbow trout out of the deeps. A café provides refreshments and views out over the lake.

ST BREWARD (SX096765) (B5)

This long drawn out village is in fact made up of four or five settlements, from Limehead in the south to the Churchtown at the top end. It is a mixture of old granite cottages and modern bungalows, many enjoying the wonderful views that come with living on an escarpment. The centre of the village is at Row where you will find the Post Office and village shop, the shop also has a small tourist information display tucked away in the right hand corner at the back.

Although mining was carried out in the area in the 1800s, it was through granite quarrying that the village developed. Today, all the local quarries except DeLank are closed down Tor Down, just below the village, closed towards the end of the 1990s but has recently reopened on a small scale, reusing the waste stone built up over the years.

Said to be the highest church in Cornwall (in altitude not height), St Breward Church is virtually the last building in the village. Parts of the chancel date back to Norman times, but much of what can be seen nowadays is the result of restoration work done in the mid 1800s. This was done under the supervision of JP St Aubyn, who also worked on many other churches in Cornwall around the same time. His "work" was heavily criticised by the poet Sir John Betjeman who believed he had destroyed more than he had saved.

Just below the church is the Old Inn, claimed to date back to the 11th century; no one really knows how old the Old Inn is, the earliest mention of it only going back as far as 1806.

Other points of interest nearby:

Gam Bridge (SX088778) A relatively modern bridge built to replace the original which was destroyed by the great flood of 1847. The flood was the result of a sudden downpour on moorland to the north. It was reported that a wall of water, up to 18 feet higher than the usual water level, sped down the Camel Valley, washing away everything in its path, including nearly every bridge.

Holy Well (SX091768) Lying in the valley below the village, is the little well dedicated to Branwalader, the pre-Latin name for St Breward. The well was restored in Victorian times and the waters are supposed to cure itchy eyes. It is thought a chapel once stood nearby.

ST CLEER (SX248683) (G8)

The village of St Cleer sits on the southern edge of a large parish of over 11,000 acres, much of which is open moorland. Parts of the church, a notable landmark in the surrounding countryside, date back to Norman times although much of the building, including the tower, date from the 15th century. In a parish whose population grew from just under 1000 in 1831 to just under 4000 thirty years later, it is not surprising to find several non-conformist chapels. With the miners who made up much of the population at the time long gone, the chapels have fallen into disrepair and are now closed or converted into homes. The small Dissenter's Chapel on the road out of the village to the north is still open occasionally to visitors in search of family history, the building itself surrounded by the graves of many of the miners and their families. The Liskeard and Caradon railway line ran along the bottom edge of the graveyard as part of its circuitous route up to the mines on Caradon Hill.

Between the church and the Dissenters Chapel is the village's Holy Well. One of the most famous on the moor, it was rebuilt in 1864 and now stands in its own little courtyard adjacent to a cross. At one time, lunatics were immersed in the water in the hope that they would be cured but a grill over the pool now prevents this.

Other points of interest nearby:

Tremar and Tremar Coombe (SX255685) Spread along the side of a tributary of the Seaton River, the Tremars, like other hamlets in the area, developed through the success of mining. Today, although some of the original miners' cottages remain, there is a proliferation of modern bungalows, slowly reaching out to join up with St Cleer on the hillside above. The old Methodist Chapel, although no longer used for worship, still takes centre stage in Tremar Coombe.

St Cleer Well

ST CLETHER (SX206844) (F2)

Dissected by the River Inny, the parish of St Clether sits to the north of the moor and is made up of scattered farmsteads. At its centre sits the church, rebuilt in the late 1800s after being destroyed by fire in 1865. The vicarage opposite is said to be the inspiration for Thomas Hardy's poem 'The Face at the Casement' about his wife's ex-boyfriend.

A short walk from the church leads to St Clether Holy Well and Chapel, the largest of its type in Cornwall. The site is thought to have originated in the 6th century when Clederus, one of Brechin of Wales' 24 children, set up a hermitage in the valley. By the 15th century the building had fallen into disrepair and was renovated, a process repeated in the late 1800s. The large altar is believed to date from the 15th Century, whilst a plaque resting against the wall dates from 1913 and asks visitors to

The small chapel at St Clether with the well house behind

place 3d in the box for the upkeep of the building. Unless you have a threepennybit on you, I would suggest leaving a slightly larger donation.

Across the valley sits Basill Manor, built in the 16th century and for a long time the home of the Trevelyan family. It is now a residential home for autistic adults, with their own farm and craft workshops.

ST NEOT (SX185678) (E8)

Snuggled into its own little valley on the southern edge of the moor, the village of St Neot hides from the fact that its parish, the second largest in Cornwall, contains vast areas of high moorland. Behind the church, on south facing slopes, green patchworks of fields stretch off into the distance. Below, the Loveny (or St Neot) River, meanders through meadows on its way to the join the River Fowey at Twowatersfoot. On the edge of one of these meadows sits St Neot Holy Well, where the saint is supposed to have caught his daily meal of one fish. He found the area a perfect place to live, and to many it keeps its appeal. In 2002 it was judged the village of the year for south and south-west England and then took the national title in 2004.

The saint after whom the village is named has origins open to argument. Could he

The Story of St George is told in this window in St Neot Church

have been a Celtic saint, also connected with the village of Menheniot east of Liskeard, or is he the Saxon relative of King Alfred who left Glastonbury to seek solitude in Cornwall? The experts seem to have come to the conclusion that St Neot is a combination of the two and his story, told in wonderful detail by stained glass windows in the church, is well worth viewing.

It is not just the story of St Neot that adorns the church windows, both the Creation and the legend of St George and the Dragon are represented, with others, and are said to be amongst the finest 16th century windows of their type in the whole of the UK.

Outside the church there are several early crosses to view. Those looking up will see an oak branch sticking out from the top of the tower. This signifies the villagers' Royalist support during the English Civil War, and every 29th May (Oak Apple Day) the branch is replaced.

Next door to the church is the London Inn, a popular watering hole and also handy for a spot of lunch. The name derives from when St Neot was on the main coaching route between Bodmin, Liskeard and beyond.

The Doorstep Green is an open area near the river where villagers have created a pleasant community space with terraced gardens and an amphitheatre.

Other points of interest nearby:

Carnglaze Caverns (SX187668) Like most villages around the edge of the moor, St Neot had a mining

industry in the mid 1800s. Very little remains to be seen and it is a different type of extraction industry that brings visitors to the area now. Carnglaze is a disused underground slate quarry that is open to the public with guided tours available. During the Second World War the navy used the cavern to store surplus rum, and nowadays "The Rum Store" is used to host underground music concerts.

TEMPLE (SX146733) (D6)

Now bypassed by the A30 and no longer a separate parish, the little hamlet of Temple has avoided modern development.

Temple Church, hidden away in the centre of the moor

The church, hidden away even by Temple standards, sits on the edge of a valley that feeds the Bedalder River. It was originally founded in the 12th century by the Knights Templar who built a hospice for travellers braving the tracks across the moor. By the 18th century, the church had fallen into disrepair and, in 1883, it was completely rebuilt to the original design.

The area around Temple saw a small China Clay industry grow up in the 1870s, developed by a man called Frank Parkyn. Hawk's Tor and Glynn Valley, to the north and south respectively, were the most successful, but smaller works such as Burnt Heath and Temple to the west also provided much needed employment in the centre of the moor.

Other points of interest nearby:
See also CARDINHAM MOOR

TOLBOROUGH TOR
(SX175778) (E4)

Overlooking Jamaica Inn to the south, Tolborough is seldom visited despite its proximity to one of the moor's biggest tourist attractions. On its summit sits a large cairn, built so that it incorporates the natural rocks, and from here the view north towards Brown Willy and Roughtor is one of pure wild moorland.

Trethevy Quoit

A standing stone on the hill's eastern flank may not be as old as it looks, whilst in the valley to the north, towards Catshole Tor, sits a long cairn. One of only three on the moor, this boat shaped scattering of stones could be 5000 yrs old.

TREGARRICK TOR
(SX242713) (G7)

Sitting at the end of a ridge leading west from Craddock Moor, Tregarrick looks down onto Siblyback Lake. Crowned with a jumbled pile of rock and surrounded by prehistoric remains, it is impossible to know what role this crag had in former times. A line of cairns lead back across the open moorland towards Stowe's Hill, passing through the Craddock Moor stone circle, whilst the gorse bushes on the western flank hide a standing stone.

Although close to Siblyback Lake, the tor is best approached from Minions.

TRETHEVY QUOIT
(SX259687) (H8)

Hidden behind hedges and houses, this antiquity can be easily missed. It is one of Cornwall's oldest man made structures with some experts dating its construction to 4,500 B.C. Known as a portal dolmen, this burial chamber may have been constructed to house the remains of not just one person, but many over a period of time. As with so many of the antiquities dotted around Cornwall, any evidence of its use had been removed long before archaeologists were "invented", but it is still a fascinating place to visit.

TREWINT (SX220805) (F3)

Wesley's cottage at Trewint

This little village was for many years cut in two by the busy A30. Now by-passed, it is a quiet place visited mainly by those making a pilgrimage to a little cottage down Duck Street. Here, in the mid 1700s, a local man, Digory Isbell, built an extension on to his home so that John Wesley, the Methodist preacher, could have somewhere to stay whilst on his travels into deepest Cornwall. Since the 1950s the cottage has been open to the public, and contains fascinating displays on all things "methodical".

TWELVE MEN'S MOOR
(SX250753) (H5)

This unusual name dates back to the 13th century when the priory at Launceston made an agreement with the twelve tenants who farmed the area between the Withybrook and the Lynher River. It includes the windswept tors of Kilmar, Hawk's, Trewortha, Bearah and Sharp Tor, some of the most rugged and beautiful scenery on the moor.

Hawk's Tor, as seen from the lower slopes of Kilmar Tor

The northerly ridges of Hawk's Tor and Trewortha are possibly the least visited, partly due to heavy use of barbed wire around Hawk's Tor. However, both are on open access land, although Trewortha can be closed off at certain times of the year. It is on Trewortha Tor that King Arthur's Bed can be found, a naturally carved rock basin shaped so that a knight could sleep undetected.

Bearah, sitting between Sharp Tor and Kilmar, is a small tor eaten into on the south side by quarrying. A stoneworks is still in operation, although quarrying has stopped, and all around the site are the remains of failed projects or off-cuts of finished works. Please be careful if visiting whilst work is taking place.

A track leads from the quarry down towards Blackcoombe Farm. Halfway down it passes a chambered cairn on the left, the large stones mostly fallen and often hidden by ferns.

See also, Sharp Tor, Kilmar Tor.

UPTON CROSS (SX281721) (J7)

Small community on the B3254 Liskeard Launceston road where it is crossed by the road from the low lying farmland to the east, up on to the high moorland around Minions. The village supports a thriving school, Post Office and church and is the home to Sterts Theatre. Here seasonal performances take place in an amphitheatre covered by a large umbrella style roof. The remains of the mining boom of the 1800s can be seen from footpaths all around the village but, due to their state of disrepair, many of the buildings should not be entered.

Other points of interest nearby:

Rilla Mill (SX295732) Sitting astride the Lynher River to the east of the moor, this has been an important crossing point since early times and it is thought that a bridge existed here in 1170. Just upstream is Starabridge, thought by Cornish historian Charles Henderson to be one of the most picturesque bridges in the county.

WARLEGGAN (SX157690) (D8)

The small village of Warleggan sits hidden

from the masses, rarely visited except by fans of the Winston Graham Poldark novels or those seeking out the church and the story of its former parson. He was the Reverend Densham and it was Daphne du Maurier's version of his time in the village that draws people there. He was, if we believe her words, an eccentric man who fell out with all his parishioners to the point that he erected cardboard effigies in the church just to have someone to preach to. The reasons for his falling out with the parishioners are many - but was he eccentric or just out of place amongst people not used to outsiders?

Local sources suggest he was not quite as "strange" as du Maurier made out and putting aside her story, the church is a pleasant place to visit, tucked away up a short tree lined drive. It is a low solid building which at one time had a spire, until lightning destroyed it in 1818. The building to the right of the church is known locally as the band-room, but is thought to have been built originally by a French priest as a brewhouse in the early 1700s.

WENFORDBRIDGE
(SX085752) (A6)

Crossing the River Camel, this bridge is just upstream from the china clay dries that gave the Bodmin and Wenford railway its name. From here china clay would be taken by rail to Bodmin to join the main line. This all ended in the early 1980s and now the route is part of the Camel Trail for cyclists and walkers. The kilns that dried the china clay were opened in 1906 with the clay being piped down from the Stannon works near Roughtor. Today, the trail runs along the front of the works.

The bridge, like all but Helland, was destroyed in the great flood of 1847 and rebuilt later. Nearby was the former Wenford Inn which in the 1930s became the Wenford Bridge Pottery run by Michael Cardew and later his son Seth. This has now closed.

WEST MOOR (SX195805) (E3)

For some strange reason West Moor is on the northeast side of the moor and comprises of a large relatively featureless area of Altarnun parish. It is one of the few wild parts of the moor to be crossed by footpaths, hinting back to an earlier time before the A30 was the main route across the moor.

Evidence of tin streaming and peat cutting can be found, whilst a stone circle has been discovered in recent years just north of Westmoorgate.

To the south, on Hendra Downs is the conical hill known as the Beacon, on its southern flank is the Elephant Rock, thought to have been left perched in its position in some distant ice age.

See also, Bray Down, Leskernick.

BODMIN MOOR
Flora and fauna

Bodmin Moor lies at an altitude of between 250 metres (800 feet) and 420 metres (1,300 feet), from the low marshes to the heights of Brown Willy. It is easily noticeable, even to the most unobservant visitor, that, apart from the modern conifer plantations, there are very few trees. Instead the moor is populated rather by shrubs and bushes, such as gorse, heather and the occasional wind battered blackthorn. Here and there, in sheltered valleys, ancient woodland, predominantly oak, provides a habitat for rare lichens, liverworts, mosses and ferns.

In the wetter areas, sphagnum, or bog moss can be found. This delicate habitat is home to insectivorous sundews and butterworts, as well as bog bean and bog asphodel, amongst others. The heath grass grows in large clumps amongst the bogs or on the edge of open water as does purple moor grass. Midsummer on the moor would not be the same without the white feathery tufts of cotton grass. Found in the damper areas, King Arthur's Hall being a good spot, the sight of the clumps of grass waving in a breeze under a blue sky beats any formal flower display.

The keen botanist will be kept busy searching out the flora on different parts of the moor. The heathland of the upper moor is seen as important for its rare flora and fauna, including Sundew, Common Cotton Grass and Cross-leaved Heather. There are also hundreds of rare ferns and mosses dotted across the landscape.

For those of us who are lucky enough to walk the moor regularly, there follows a list of the flora that may be found across the moor. It is by no means complete.

Red Campion

Orchid

Cotton Grass

Bogbean

Bugle – flowers May to July

Butterwort and Sundew

Common Polypody – grows on rocks, tree trunks and ground.

Cotton Grass

Devil's Bit Scabious

Early Purple Orchid

Gorse

Heath/Moorland Spotted Orchid

Heathers

Lichens

Potentilla Erecta Tormentil

Ragged Robin

Red Campion

Sphagnum Moss

Wood Anemone

Wood-Sorrel – flowers April to June, flowers and leaves close up at night.

Shpagnum

The restricted habitat on the high moor means that butterflies are few with just the Small Heath being seen in any great numbers, mainly around midsummer. Moths are more common, especially the Double Line and the day flying Beautiful Yellow Underwing.

To see a better variety it is worth seeking out the wetter parts of the moor, the marshland, streams and around the reservoirs. Here can be found several types of dragon and damselfly, plus chasers, the dragonfly's stumpy relation. Hawk moths may be seen as light descends. During the day the Marsh Fritillary, a rare but very important species in Cornwall, may be spotted, especially during May and June.

Marsh Fritillary

Sundew

Gorse

BIRDS OF BODMIN MOOR
by Dawn Roberts

The following are all species that are to be seen on the Moor, although not unique to moorland. The list is not exhaustive as, with the exception of the starling, I've not included species that are common in most habitats and known to most people, such as Robin and Blue Tit. Neither have I included species that are rare or difficult to find, such as Willow Tit and Snipe. This is intended as a snap-shot of species that observant visitors to the moor should be able to see with little effort, and includes residents, passage migrants, summer visitors and winter visitors.

COMMON GOLDENEYE
Oct - Mar
Bucephala clangula

The goldeneye is mainly a winter visitor to Cornwall, although a few also pass through on migration. Up to 5 or 6 individuals regularly winter on areas of open water such as Dozmary Pool, Colliford Lake and Crowdy Reservoir. Both sexes have the prominent yellow eye which gives this species its name. The goldeneye is smaller than the much commoner mallard, and is a diving duck whereas the mallard dabbles and upends to feed. The male goldeneye is a strikingly handsome bird with a dark, glossed green head, which appears black from a distance, with a large white spot below the eye. Upperparts are black and white, whilst underparts are white. The female has a brown head, white neck ring and mottled grey body. In flight, both sexes reveal a white inner wing.

COMMON BUZZARD
Jan - Dec
Buteo buteo

The buzzard is a large bird of prey that is a common resident in the western half of Britain. Sexes are alike but plumage varies from dark brown (dark phase) to creamy white (pale phase). Since this species is often viewed from below as it soars on broad wings, or perches in the open, the

Common Goldeneye

Common Buzzard

of up to 1,000 strong spend the winter here. Favoured habitats are moors, heaths, marshes and open fields. They are regular in their habits and, if seen once in a given area, they're likely to be encountered there again year on year. On Bodmin Moor the Colliford/Dozmary and Crowdy/Davidstow areas are reliable sites. The golden plover is about the size of a blackbird, albeit with longer legs. Sexes are alike and, in winter plumage, they have a golden hue to their upperparts, white underparts, and a lightly streaked, buffy breast. The bill is short, thin and black, and the legs are dark grey.

underside is seen more often than the upperparts – in all colour phases, look for a heavily barred tail, dark breast, dark carpal patches (elbows) and dark wing tips. The buzzard is a solitary species although small numbers soar together. This is often when the distinctive high-pitched 'pee-oo' call may be heard as they communicate with each other.

EUROPEAN GOLDEN PLOVER
Sep - Mar

Pluvialis apricaria

The golden plover is an upland breeding species with the nearest confirmed breeding area being Dartmoor. Large numbers pass through Cornwall on migration and flocks

Golden Plover

NORTHERN LAPWING
Oct - Mar
Vanellus vanellus

Northern Lapwing

The lapwing got its name from its laboured (lapping) flight. It is also known as the green plover, due to its dark green upperparts, and pee-wit, due to its plaintive call. It is a common breeding species over most of Britain but it is a scarce breeder in Cornwall. However, large numbers winter here, often sharing habitat with their relatives the golden plover, with whom they form large, mixed flocks. Sexes are alike, and the distinctive plumage is the same all year – green upperparts, black wings, black breast, white belly and rump, black tail band and rust undertail. The face and head are black and white with a distinctive wispy crest. The bill is short, thin and black, and the long legs are dark red.

COMMON CUCKOO
Apr- Sep
Cuculus canorus

The cuckoo is often heard but seldom seen. It is a passage migrant and brief summer visitor to Britain. Once here it attracts a mate with its distinctive call and proceeds to find a host nest, after which it makes its way back to Africa again. Since the meadow pipit is one of the host species, the cuckoo may be seen wherever the pipit is seen. On Bodmin Moor, a reliable site in May is the Sharptor/Kilmar Tor area, near Henwood. Whilst the male is always grey, the female may be seen in 2 morphs – grey

Common Cuckoo

or brown. But, apart from the call, the most diagnostic feature is the long tail and habit of drooping its wings when perched.

COMMON SKYLARK
Jan - Dec
Alauda arvensis

Although seen throughout the county, the skylark is symbolic of Bodmin Moor where it nests on the ground. Walkers and horse-riders will often see and hear the skylark ascend quickly and retreat low over the ground. It may then ascend and hover in the air, constantly calling. This is often because they're close to the nest and the adult is trying to draw attention away from the fragile construction and its precious contents. Like the meadow pipit, the skylark's plumage is a fairly nondescript brown. But, the slightly larger skylark has prominent dark streaks on the upperparts, a thicker bill and the hint of a crest. The skylark is much more vocal and aerial than the meadow pipit and doesn't have its characteristic jerky gait.

MEADOW PIPIT
Jan - Dec
Anthus pratensis

The meadow pipit is a house-sparrow sized bird that breeds and over-winters in Cornwall, as well as passing through in large numbers in the autumn (Sept/Oct). It is a busy little bird, always rushing

Common Skylark

Meadow Pipet

around in its search for food, tail constantly wagging. Its plumage is fairly nondescript – the upperparts and breast are buffy with dark brown streaking, whilst the belly and throat are white. The legs are orange/pink and the brown bill is short and thin. This species is generally solitary but it can occasionally be seen in flocks of up to 50. The meadow pipit's nest is one of many that are parasitized by the cuckoo.

WHEATEAR
Mar - Oct
Oenanthe oenanthe

The wheatear is a summer migrant from Africa, where it spends the British

Wheatear

winter. It is about the size of a robin and is conspicuous in its habit of perching on vantage points such as boulders and hedges. The male has a blue/grey back, buff breast, white underparts and a prominent black eye-stripe. In the female the blue/grey is replaced with warm brown, and the eye-stripe is less prominant. Both sexes have dark wings, a black and white tail and black bare parts. In flight the white rump is distinctive and many people believe that 'wheatear' is a corruption of an earlier name for this species: 'white arse'. Bodmin Moor is the breeding stronghold for this species in Cornwall.

FIELDFARE
Oct - Mar
Turdus pilaris

The fieldfare is a passage migrant and winter visitor to Cornwall. On Bodmin Moor it is commonly seen around the Colliford/Dozmary area, often in mixed flocks with redwing and, sometimes, mistle thrush. It is a blackbird-sized thrush with a grey crown and rump, chestnut-brown upperparts and black tail. The belly is plain white whilst the flanks and ochre breast are speckled. Its yellow bill is short and thin, and the legs are black.

Fieldfare

REDWING
Oct - Mar

Turdus iliacus

Like the fieldfare, with which it is often seen, the redwing is a passage migrant and winter visitor to Cornwall. It is slightly smaller than the song thrush and, if seen briefly, may be mistaken for one because both species have brown upperparts and white speckled under parts. However, the redwing has bold facial markings and rufous flanks which separate it from the song thrush. The most prominent facial feature is a bold, creamy eyebrow. If a 'song thrush' is disturbed from a berry-producing tree in winter, and followed by another, and then another, each one giving a soft 'seeip' call, it is almost certainly a redwing and not a song thrush, which is more solitary in its habits.

MISTLE THRUSH
Jan - Dec

Turdus viscivorus

In Cornwall, the mistle thrush is a breeding resident with the population increasing during passage and over the winter. At first glance, it is like a larger, greyer, more upright song thrush with rounded black spots, as opposed to arrowheads, on the

Redwing

Mistle Thrush

COMMON STARLING
Jan - Dec

Sturnus vulgaris

The starling, although a common garden bird known to everyone, deserves a place in this section on account of its spectacular large flocks, especially in winter when resident numbers are swelled by winter visitors. The Roughtor/Crowdy area is one of many sites where starlings may be seen going to roost in their thousands. Since this species has declined in recent years, and milder winters mean less winter visitors, flocks are smaller than in the past. In 1991 one observer commented that the Crowdy roost contained "millions, too many to count". Nonetheless, a flock of starlings going to roost at sunset on a winter's evening, with the backdrop of Roughtor, is a magical sight and sound not to be missed.

underparts. From bill to tail it is about the size of a blackbird, but appears larger on account of its rotund belly. This is also apparent when seen on its undulating flight. It is less tame than the song thrush and, when disturbed, it gives a football rattle-like alarm call and flies off. Since this species is often found at higher elevations, Bodmin Moor is a reliable site, where singles, pairs and flocks of up to a dozen are regularly seen.

Common Starling

MAMMALS ON BODMIN MOOR
by Clive ffitch

There are many mammals to be found on Bodmin Moor but not all of them are as obvious and easily spotted as others! There are many free-roaming animals that are a vital part of the working nature and environment of the moor, including sheep, cattle and ponies. All of these animals need to be respected, and care must always be taken when driving along moorland lanes where many animals graze beside the verge or, indeed, walk on the road.

Dogs must always be kept on a lead whenever livestock is around, and by law at all times between 1st March and 31st July (lambing time and breeding time for ground nesting birds).

If you happen to see a young mammal or a bird that seems to have been abandoned, it is always best to leave it well alone, as its parent is very likely nearby or watching it. Any young animal or bird that is interfered with by humans will lessen its chance of survival in the wild.

OTTER

Surprisingly the most recorded mammal species in Cornwall, having a high profile, and popular with both the public and conservationists. The otter is now common on most Cornish rivers, including the Fowey to the south of the moor and the Camel to the west, but casual sightings are rare.

DEER

The Roe Deer is a native deer, and is relatively common over the whole of East Cornwall, with an even distribution over Bodmin Moor. Red Deer are also native,

but are far less common; and the Fallow Deer which were originally introduced to parkland by the Normans for hunting (and some possibly even by the Romans), are even rarer, having only been sighted on the southern fringes of the moor.

BADGER

Badgers are common on and around the edge of the moor, with numbers increasing. They are nocturnal, and are omnivores, eating mainly earthworms, but also small mammals, insects, berries, fruit and other vegetation. Their large setts can be built over generations and sometimes contain over 1km of tunnels.

RED FOX

Although mainly nocturnal, foxes can often be seen walking across the wilder parts of the moor. They are easily adaptable and will eat almost anything, storing any surplus food for later.

BATS

The Greater Horseshoe bat, now restricted in the UK to the far southwest, can often be found roosting in the mine adits on the edge of the moor. They emerge at dusk in the summer months to feed on flying beetles and moths, and can often be seen dashing across meadows at this time. Other bats that may be found on, or around the moor, include the Brown Long-eared bat, the Lesser Horseshoe and Daubenton's.

Many mine adits and shafts have been closed off by grills, preventing human entry to important breeding habitats for these endangered mammals.

PONIES

Unlike Dartmoor, there are no specifically defined breeds of ponies on Bodmin Moor. Many are left out on the moor to fend for themselves, being rounded up in the autumn for the sales at Hallworthy Livestock Market. Do not attempt to feed them.

SHEEP

The favoured sheep breeds on the moor used to be Cornwall Longwools and Dartmoors, but since the 1930s, Scottish Blackface and North Country Cheviots have become more common. Left to roam across the open moor, sheep are often seen with

1950s, a number of hardy Scottish breeds have become a popular sight on the moor. These include pure Highland cattle, with their distinctive horns, Galloways, and Blue Greys.

WILD CATS

Sightings of big cats, known locally as the 'Beast of Bodmin Moor', have been allegedly witnessed on and off over the last 20 years or so. The Panther, likely the black 'melanistic' Panther, or perhaps the Puma, are possibly the rarest mammals ever sighted on the moor, and are definitely an introduced species. In the 1970s, after the introduction of the Wild Animals Act, it is believed several large cats were released into the wild. Bodmin Moor would have been a particularly suitable location, and there are many hidden corners where large breeding cats could live unnoticed for many years. However, very few of the possible sightings have ever been confirmed and reports over the last ten years have been minimal.

dyed fleeces. This identifies them to their owners when it is time to bring them back to enclosed land. Sheep creeps, small gaps built into moorland walls, can still be seen in places. These allow sheep to pass through, but larger animals like cattle can not.

CATTLE

Most of the cattle seen on the moor will be bred for beef; the production of milk on any scale being a shortlived industry during the 1930s when the Milk Marketing Board gave out subsidies to farmers. Since the